'*Fresh Pathways in Prayer* stands out for its wise blend of personal honesty with biblical truth. It makes prayer, which can seem an unattainable ideal, into a practical resource. If you want to pray but feel defeated before you even begin, Julian Hardyman's faithful guidance here can help you.'
Ray Ortlund, pastor, Immanuel Church, Nashville, Tennessee

'This short book will be a tonic to new and mature Christians alike – anyone who feels their prayer life needs some encouragement and energy. This is a great little book, simultaneously practical and profound. Drawing on biblical patterns of prayer along with a careful selection of Christian spirituality across the centuries, Julian Hardyman offers a dozen or so simple things that you can do as you pray. But, if done in the context of faith, they will lead you into a deeper, richer relationship with God. There is something here to freshen up the prayer life of every believer. I'm looking forward to re-reading it and putting it into practice.'
Tim Chester, pastor of Grace Church Boroughbridge and faculty member of Crosslands Training

'For any Christian who longs to deepen their relationship and experience of God, yet who, at times, struggles to pray, this book will be of unequalled benefit. In his characteristically honest style, Julian walks us through the difficult paths of prayer we invariably tread and then offers wonderfully insightful biblical and practical ideas to help us find Fresh Pathways in Prayer. I am convinced this little book far outweighs its size in honesty and wisdom and will change the prayer life of every one of its readers.'
Val Archer, pastor's wife, speaker and member of Chessington Evangelical Church and The Globe Church, London.

'Julian Hardyman shows a deep understanding of the human heart and an abundance of real-life wisdom that can only have come from a veteran pastor whose own prayer life is genuine, honest, and deep, but not without struggles of his own. I found much fresh insight in his remarkably practical, helpful, biblically-anchored book. Highly recommended!'
Wayne Grudem, Professor of Theology and Biblical Studies Phoenix Seminary, Arizona

D1494916

FRESH PATHWAYS
IN PRAYER

JULIAN HARDYMAN

FRESH

PATHWAYS

IN PRAYER

10 Publishing
a division of 10 of those.com

Copyright © 2019 by Julian Hardyman

First published in Great Britain in 2019

British Library Cataloguing in Publication Data
A record for this book is available from the British Library

ISBN: 978-1-912373-66-6

Designed by Jordan Cox at The TreeFish

Printed in Denmark by Nørhaven

10Publishing, a division of 10ofthose.com
Unit C, Tomlinson Road, Leyland, PR25 2DY, England
Email: info@10ofthose.com
Website: www.10ofthose.com

To two dear friends and colleagues in ministry:
Peter Lewis and Peter Comont

Contents

Acknowledgements

I am so grateful to friends who have read this and made comments, especially the ever-helpful Amy Donovan who has done so much to improve my writing over the years. I am also indebted to Julie Hatherall for her expert editing and to the wonderful folk at 10ofThose for taking on the project. My beloved wife, Debbie, made it possible for me to spend time away from home for writing. The quality of her own prayer life has very evidently grown through the years and impresses me day after day after day. My children, Robin, Fiona and Kitty, continually inspire me with their commitment to Christ.

Introduction: When I feel stuck

How does this imaginary dialogue between two Christians sound to you?

> *Prayer is the way we express the personal relationship we have with God through Jesus. So, just talk to God.*
>
> Well, yes, praying is talking to God … so I should talk to God.
>
> *And?*
>
> I am not sure how to put this.
>
> *Go on.*
>
> I can't see him.
>
> *No.*
>
> And to be honest, I can't hear him either. I know lots of Christians talk about listening to God and hearing him speak. But I am not sure how to listen and am pretty sure I don't hear him speak.
>
> *[silence]*
>
> And because I can't see or hear him, it isn't really like a conversation I have with another person – not even one on Messenger or WhatsApp. It's, well, it's just very different.

I'm still with you.

And so often I feel as though I am talking to myself – or to nobody.

[silence]

And so often it gets … [embarrassed smile] a bit predictable and even …

[long pause]

Boring?

Well, you said it, not me. But yes, a bit dull! I seem to say roughly the same things every day and nothing much changes. I wonder if anything is really happening at all!

What would you say in this conversation? I know plenty of people who would identify pretty strongly with the second speaker. They struggle with prayer – and find it hard to talk about it. Is it a taboo? Or is it that everyone assumes that they are the only one who feels like this while everyone else has it sorted?

Plenty of quite mature Christians struggle with prayer – they find what they do unrewarding, or they do very little praying. This book is intended to help those folk.

But it is not just for those who are struggling to pray at all. It is also for people who do pray but feel a bit stuck in a routine, particularly one of reading a Bible passage, working out what it means and then working through some prayers for the day and for other people. If that is you, then this is a great practice – and one that many Christians would love to have – but I know that you want more. I hope you will find in what follows some ideas for going deeper in prayer, particularly prayer as the expression of our relationship with God and one of the main ways we experience God.

This book should be helpful too for new(ish) Christians who do not know quite where to begin with prayer or really what to do!

Questions

How much do you identify with the person who really struggles to pray at all? Or perhaps you relate to the one who does pray but finds it a bit of a routine and not much else?

Prayer

Lord, I guess you must be working in me or I wouldn't be reading this. I do want to pray more or for my prayer to be less routine. Will you show me? Amen

---

1

When I don't know how to get (re-)started

If you are not praying very much at all on your own, you need to know that you are not the only one. It is more common than you think. That doesn't make it a good place to be of course and I suspect you aren't altogether happy with it – or you wouldn't bother with a book on prayer. Or perhaps you are a newish Christian and wondering how to get going.

I want to suggest something very simple and basic to help you to get (re-)started. Pray the Lord's Prayer once a day because that is Jesus' model prayer for his followers. You probably know a version of the words by heart. If not, here is one which you can use:

Our Father in heaven
Hallowed be your name
Your kingdom come
Your will be done
On earth as it is in heaven
Give us this day our daily bread
Forgive us our sin as we forgive those who sin against us
Lead us not into temptation but deliver us from evil
For yours is the kingdom, the power and the glory
For ever and ever
Amen.

You might want to write it out on a card or make a screenshot of it for your phone so it is accessible until you do know it by heart. My recommendation is to say it every day for a week.

Prayer for a Christian is talking to God as your Father. Note the capital 'F'. This is of course what Jesus did.[1] And we can do that too because Jesus, through his life, death and resurrection, has brought us into his family as his brothers and sisters (Hebrews 2:11 tells us that Jesus loves calling us his brothers and sisters!). So we adopt his posture – praying to God as Father. This is our basic theology of prayer. Prayer is not writing 'help' on a piece of paper, putting it in a bottle and throwing it out to sea in the hope that someone will read it and do something. Prayer is talking to a heavenly Father in the total security of being in his family.

Our prayer involves the Holy Spirit too:

Because you are his sons, God sent the Spirit of his Son into our hearts, the Spirit who calls out, 'Abba, Father' (Galatians 4:6).

The Spirit you received brought about your adoption to sonship. And by him we cry, 'Abba, Father.' The Spirit himself testifies with our spirit that we are God's children (Romans 8:15b–16).

So it is the Holy Spirit who leads us into that childlike posture towards God. We say 'Father' but actually it is the Holy Spirit speaking too! We do so because of his presence and work.

We go on to say, 'Hallowed be your name' because the most important person is not us but God. What matters more than any of our needs is that he should be honoured as holy – and that his rule (his kingdom) should grow and that his desires (his will) be done as much on this earth as they are in heaven. As we say these words, we align our will with his will.

But that does not mean that our needs are irrelevant to him. We can and should bring them all to him in prayer. So we ask for our practical needs: 'Give us this day our daily bread.' We bring them to him day-by-day in confidence and trust. We present our spiritual needs too, first looking back: 'Forgive us our sin as we forgive those who sin against us.' We can pray that in total assurance that we will be forgiven instantly, totally and freely. Secondly, we mention our spiritual needs looking forward: 'Lead us not into temptation but deliver us from evil.' We pray that to acknowledge that we can't fight the battles of the Christian life alone but that God can give us all we need to do so.

We finish with the beautiful ending the church has added to the words of Jesus: 'For yours is the kingdom, the power and the glory, For ever and ever. Amen.'

Let's bring this back to the struggle to pray very much at all and my suggestion that you pray the Lord's Prayer every day for a week. Even if you pray only the first line – or even only the first two words, 'Our Father' – something amazing and supernatural will have happened. Your 'Our Father' will be the vocalised expression of who you really are: a new child of God speaking to his or her Father in heaven. It is the voice of the new creation underway in you. You may be just dimly aware of it but it is no less real for that. To you it is two words, perhaps quite hard to say if you come from a starting point of dryness and dullness and even guilt. To God it is one small but beautiful part of his supernatural work in your life, deeply pleasing to him because that is what he sent his Son to create.

This is our basic theology of prayer. We are talking to our Father because he invites us to. We need have no fear or hesitation because the finished work of Christ means that all the barriers are removed and we are part of his family. We have an all-powerful Protector who looks on us with compassion like the kindest of fathers or mothers. He answers our prayers with great wisdom, always taking the long-term view of what is best for us and his kingdom.[2]

Having given you that practical suggestion, I want to follow it with a few more which I have found helpful when I am not praying much at all:

- *The less you pray, the harder it is.[3]*
  Prayer is subject to many natural laws in human life and this is one of them. If you are struggling to pray, you may be the victim of your own vicious circle; in fact you almost certainly have been because we all do this. This insight won't solve the problem but you need to realise it. The great thing is that the opposite is also true: the more you pray, the more natural it will become.

- *Prayer can become a habit and different kinds of prayer can become habitual.*
  When I moved town for my first job, I started attending a church on Sundays. One Wednesday evening I went along

to the weekly church prayer meeting. The next Sunday the pastor, Gary, said how glad he had been to see me at the prayer meeting and added, 'I hope you'll make it a habit.' I did and it was a good habit to develop. There are dangers with reducing our relationship with God (or anyone else) into just a set of habits. But if your starting point is hardly praying at all, that is your current habit and you should develop a new one!

• *Work out how to bring in others to help.*
Many people (though not all) find it easier to pray with others. We'll be exploring that a bit more in a later chapter. If that is you, perhaps you need to find someone else to pray with regularly so that can be the launch pad for you to pray more on your own. Or perhaps you just need to talk to someone about your struggles and seek their support. You could even invite them to regularly ask how you are finding prayer. In short you may not be able to relaunch your prayer life on your own but do not despair: find help and use it!

• *You will not pray unless you plan to pray.*[4]
Simply hoping that there will be an opportunity for prayer tends not to produce that space. People differ, naturally, with some liking planned and regular patterns more than others. But whatever your personality type, there are all sorts of things in your life that you already make space for and plan to do. Prayer is not exempt from the same rule. Although spontaneous prayer is a wonderful feature

of many people's prayer lives and well worth cultivating, we cannot rely on spontaneous prayer alone. It sounds a spiritual approach but it won't work on its own. Where could you set aside time to pray today?

• *Pray until you pray.*[5]
This is an insight from the Puritans. It sounds a bit paradoxical but it is really helpful. It is a bit more than 'just do it': the idea is that you may feel tentative, awkward, disengaged, embarrassed, distracted, half-hearted or even hypocritical but you should still pray. As you do that, you will find growth – because God is involved. Even the shortest and most hesitant prayers are evidence of the Holy Spirit working in you. As you pray, you are going with the flow of what he is doing at a deep, undetectable level in your being. It may not feel as though something supernatural is going on but it is. It really is.

• *Pray the prayer God gives you on any occasion.*[6]
We need to remember that prayer is not just something we do; it is a gift from God – and a gift not just in general terms but every time. Sometimes certain kinds of prayer will feel more right and natural than others and it may well be those are the kinds of prayer God wants to give us at that moment. This could seem dangerous advice but I am not saying, 'Only pray for others when you feel like it and only praise God when you feel like it.' Instead if you feel the flow of a particular kind of prayer, don't stop!

- *Be realistic, aiming for your prayer to be little and often.*
A few minutes daily may well be the best approach if you are currently struggling to pray. Five minutes a day is almost certainly much better than a 35-minute prayer binge on Sunday afternoon but nothing for the rest of the week because it keeps you much more 'anchored' and active in your relationship with God. It also provides a good base for gradual expansion to five to ten minutes a day and perhaps even to 20 minutes a day in time. But if your starting point is praying very little indeed, why not aim to say the Lord's Prayer and then add a couple of things to that each day for a week – before seeing how that builds to more.

- *Above all, tell God where you are spiritually and what you want.*
In spite of all the different reasons why you find prayer hard, actually you want things to be different, deep down, don't you? Tell God that. Tell him how you really want to pray and yet why it is so hard. You may find it is helpful for you to do this before you start praying the Lord's Prayer daily. Or a daily Lord's Prayer may be a great starting point because as you enter into the stance and posture of a child to a loving heavenly father, you may well find that you naturally have more to say to him, with prayer forming part of that.

Questions

Why not consider what you have just read and try to put your finger on what has impacted you most. Pay attention to that. Turn it over in your mind. How do you want to take it forward?

Prayer

Father, it's me here. I've not forgotten you but it must feel like that. I am not at all sure what's been going on but things have been a bit distant, haven't they? Something in me wants to say that you could have done more to draw me to you but that feels wrong and I am sure it's really my problem. What are we going to do? I've been here before and that makes it feel all the more difficult to get out of this cycle. But here's where I am at: you are what I want, even though those desires get mixed up with conflicting longings. So let's put it like this: I want to want you and I want to want you more than anything else. Please do something to help me do what I need to do. Amen.

2

When I don't know
what to say

Having started with some practical suggestions, I am going to follow with another style of praying for you to try. From quite early times in the church's history people have wanted practical guidance on prayer – not huge technical explanations but clear suggestions of what they can actually do. I want to introduce you to one approach which has been popular for centuries but has tended to be neglected in my church circles. This method is to say a short prayer – a single sentence or even just a phrase – more than once.

Immediately anyone who knows the Sermon on the Mount will rightly quote Jesus' warning in Matthew 6:

And when you pray, do not keep on babbling like pagans, for they think they will be heard because of their many words. Do not be like them, for your Father knows what you need before you ask him (Matthew 6:7–8).

Another translation, the ESV, puts it graphically:

And when you pray, do not heap up empty phrases as the Gentiles do.

But I am not at all sure that this is a command to never repeat ourselves in prayer. It is important to look at the kind of prayer Jesus is addressing above and the reason he gives. He is talking about asking God for things. He warns us not to repeat the same prayer mindlessly as if mere repetition increases the likelihood of a response. It doesn't. We don't need to think that way because God knows our needs in advance and a simple request is sufficient, though of course bringing it back to God repeatedly may be exactly what he wants.

What I am describing is a different type of praying and a different type of approach. The best way to explain it is to give an example of the type of prayer that has been used in this way throughout church history. This prayer is called the Prayer of Jesus or, more commonly, the 'Jesus Prayer', though that is rather funny way of putting it.

The wording is a single sentence, at the heart of which is the prayer of the tax collector in Jesus' parable in Luke 18:13: 'God, have mercy on me, a sinner.' But people have then applied that to Jesus, adding titles, so that he is addressed as 'Lord Jesus Christ, Son of the Living God' (all good biblical stuff!). The long version is:

> *Lord Jesus Christ*
> *Son of the Living God*
> *Have mercy on me, a sinner.*

The end of the prayer is very important – 'on me, a sinner'. It takes us back to the parable of the Pharisee and the tax collector. The tax collector stood at a distance, aware of his sin, begging for mercy. Even after we have been brought near to God in Christ, we need reminding that as sinners we are utterly dependent on his grace, that his mercy is crucial for our salvation.

Sometimes people miss out 'Lord' or 'the Living' or 'a sinner' and that's fine but I think it works best in the fullest form. The idea of how to use this is pretty simple: you pray the prayer, out loud or in your head. And you do so over and over again until it has become embedded and deeply rooted in your heart. Or as it says in Psalm 119:11, 'I have *hidden* your word in my heart that I might not sin against you' (my italics). This hiding generally only comes from repeating the verse or phrase again and again.

Rather than write more about this, the best thing would be for me to invite you to try it. If you don't want to, that's fine of course! Though I suspect you won't understand what I am saying unless you try it ...

So say the words once, slowly, obviously addressing them to Christ!

Pause.

Then say them again.

As you deliberately and slowly prayed through this prayer was there one phrase that struck you or connected with where you are at? How did it feel different to pray a set prayer if you are not used to doing that? Remember there is nothing magic about this form of words, though they are all based on biblical prayers and represent our relationship with Jesus.

You do need to say the words enough so that you have

them memorised. The repetition needed varies from person to person. I have a niece who can look at a poem and know it by heart. My dad was the same. Perhaps she got it from him. I am not like that and maybe you aren't either. But you have memorised your mobile phone number and your latest computer password (hopefully) and you can memorise this prayer. All it takes is enough repetition. Step one is to memorise it.

Then say it from memory often enough so that the words become closer and closer to the surface of your active memory. I am sure that human memories are not like pull-down menus on computer software but there are some similarities: most of us have things that are closer to the top of the menu than others.

What pops into your mind when there is a gap in proceedings? What thought pops up when something unexpected happens? Or when you wake in the night? By definition this is not under our immediate control. But nor is it totally random and by frequent usage it seems possible to put a memory higher up our list – rather in the way companies manipulate Google searches to themselves on that crucial first page.

Note that the key to making this happen is frequent usage. I am not sure that there is any other way for most of us. So if it seems right for you, you might want to aim to say the Jesus prayer five times, three times a day, for a week. I suspect you will notice some of the effects and benefits I've described if you do that, though – as I've already said – how much you need to do this will vary from person to person.

Over time people find that the Jesus Prayer has a way of humming around in the background and popping up, *helpfully*, more and more. And people find themselves thinking: 'I could pray now using the Jesus Prayer.' They then do so and end up praying much more than they used to as it is increasingly and consciously there to turn to at all sorts of moments.

Often what people find is that different parts strike them or are helpful for them in different ways at different times:

- Sometimes I am very aware of my need – I have messed up again and I need the words to say sorry and ask for forgiveness. The Jesus Prayer gives me a way of doing that (though I would never want to be limited to it, or for it to become a formula that usually tends towards paganism).

- Sometimes I may be in danger of starting the day without focusing on God at all. So if I am going to use my own words to pray, I say basically: 'Lord, please make my day trouble-free and help me get through that meeting OK.' But if when I wake I say the Jesus Prayer (or something similar – again, there is nothing magical about it), I am reminded that Jesus is my *Lord*; that God is *living* not dead; and that I need *mercy*, moment by moment.

- Sometimes I am feeling pretty good about myself. So I think my family is really rather lucky to have me as part of it; that my staff colleagues must all be so glad that I am their boss; and that on the whole the world is likely to be a better place today for my getting up and raring to go! In this situation saying the Jesus prayer can help a lot because I have to say those words 'me, a sinner.'

- At other times I am feeling the opposite: complaining to myself that it feels as though I'm the one doing all the heavy lifting at home; that no one seems to notice much what I do at church; and that the world is out to get me just because someone's cut me up in the traffic. The Jesus prayer can help a lot then too as it leads me to say those words 'me, a sinner.' They would not come onto my lips or into my mind if they were not part of a set prayer like the Jesus Prayer. But they remind me what I am, and that changes things.

Some books about the Jesus Prayer fall into two traps which I need to highlight.[1] The first is assuming that the prayer itself has some special, almost magical quality. It doesn't. The same benefits could be realised through other biblical prayers, whether composite or not. The Jesus Prayer does sum up in a wonderful way a helpful approach to Christ but to put it on a pedestal is to make it a magic formula and that is pagan. To avoid this, I would recommend finding a range of other short set words to repeat as well. More on that in a moment ...

The second danger is to use it to try to achieve a deeply calm state rather like a trance. I baulk at the idea of using Jesus' name wrongly and I do fear that sometimes either his name or this prayer can be used like a kind of mindless mantra in which content and meaning become irrelevant. You may as well be saying 'Omm' or some sort of meaningless phrase.

In addition the main goal of prayer is not achieving calmness but communicating with God. They are not the same thing! Yet, having said that, I feel a bit torn here because calming ourselves down before God is an entirely biblical idea, for example, see Psalm 131:2, 'I have calmed and quietened myself'. Using physical things like slowing our breathing down can be helpful if we are prone to agitation.

The Jesus Prayer (and other phrases or prayers that we may use this way – see below) *can* help us move into a calmer state with a conscious attentiveness to God. It seems to me that this happens as we let the words sink in at a deep level by saying them several times slowly and meaningfully.

Over time the effect builds and deepens. Human experience and consciousness seem to have several layers to them. We all experience several things going on at once. For example, we could simultaneously be driving, talking to the person in the passenger seat, thinking about what we are going to cook for dinner and have the 1970s pop song we heard in the supermarket bouncing away in our mind too. As well as that we might be going in and out of feeling a sense of sadness stemming from a conversation last night with a really upset friend. I think using the Jesus Prayer or something similar can express our relationship to God and anchor our commitment to God at different levels of our consciousness in different ways and at different times. It is really the same as memorising verses of the Bible so that they can bubble up unexpectedly and helpfully as well as being 'available' when we need them. Once again, we remember Psalm 119:11, 'I have hidden your word in my heart.'[2]

One of the benefits of this kind of repetition is that the words anchor our thoughts. This is enormously helpful when we come to try and be still and silent in the presence of God, as we will see. Another benefit is that it can help us enormously when, for all sorts of reasons, it may be hard for us to formulate our words in prayer. Illness is an obvious example. Another is tiredness. A variation on that is waking in the middle of the night. We may well want to turn from our anxious churning of thought patterns but praying with words we find for ourselves would wake us up more than feels right because we need our sleep. A friend pointed out to me that the Jesus Prayer (or something similar) can be a wonderful way of engaging with God in that situation and it's helped me on many a sleepless night since!

But I want to come back to the point made earlier that to limit ourselves to the Jesus Prayer is probably a poor idea. I encourage you to branch out! Here is how I have done that. When I was preaching sermons on Isaiah, I decided I would memorise the song of the seraphim which Isaiah heard when he saw his vision of the holiness of God in the temple:

'Holy, holy, holy is the Lord Almighty;
    the whole earth is full of his glory' (Isaiah 6:3).

I tried to recite these words when I woke up every morning that autumn. Soon I found I was wanting to say them more than once. And it was good for me that they are very different from the Jesus Prayer. They express something distinct and important.

Another set prayer that I have found helpful is this:

> *O Lord make haste to help us*
> *O Christ make speed to save us.*

The first part comes from Psalm 38:22. The whole thing is put together in the Anglican Prayer Book in the Morning and Evening Prayer services. The alliteration in 'haste / help' and 'speed / save' adds to the effect (and makes it easier to memorise). It is a bit like the Jesus Prayer and is a wonderful prayer to have at the top of your mind for those unexpected crises. When I use it on my own, I tend to say 'me' rather than 'us' at the end of each line.

A very short sentence to memorise and use is:

> *His love endures for ever.*

This comes from Psalm 136 where it is repeated 25 times (!) – a good biblical justification for repetition in prayer, I think. It acts as a kind of chorus after each mention of a different aspect of who God is or a specific mention of something he actually did for Israel. So it could be used just on its own to remind us beautifully not just of God's love but also of its never-endingness. A more developed approach is to take the chorus 'His love endures for ever' and splice it between short statements of what God has done in and for us in our life.

Yet another very helpful pattern is this three-stage prayer:

> *May the Love of Christ take hold of me (Jane/Jim)*
> *May the Love of Christ shine in my (her/his) heart*
> *May the Love of Christ flow through me (her/him) like a river.*

You pray it for yourself. Then for a loved one. Then for someone you are finding a little difficult or feeling distant from.[3]

But of course there are hundreds and thousands of possible alternatives to the Jesus Prayer, most of them simply biblical phrases.

Questions

Does this approach to prayer seem like something you would like to try? How could you develop your prayer life using the Jesus Prayer, or other biblical prayers?

Prayer

Lord Jesus Christ, Son of the Living God, have mercy on me a sinner.

Now we have got you praying with two prayers, both biblical! Why not try using both daily (and the Jesus Prayer during the day, or night, too). There are specific problems that prevent us even doing this but in the next few chapters we are going to look at ways of overcoming them.

I cannot restrain myself from also including this wonderful morning prayer as an example of a longer prayer. I have found it very helpful right at the start of the day:

A liturgy for the ritual of morning coffee

Meet me, O Christ,
in this stillness of morning.
Move me, O Spirit,
to quiet my heart.
Mend me, O Father,
from yesterday's harms.

From the discords of yesterday,
resurrect my peace.
From the discouragements of yesterday,
resurrect my hope.
From the weariness of yesterday,
resurrect my strength.
From the doubts of yesterday,
resurrect my faith.
From the wounds of yesterday,
resurrect my love.

Let me enter this new day,
aware of my need
and awake
to your grace,
O Lord.

Amen.[4]

3

When I don't feel like praising him

I have two main problems in going to church services. The first is when I am thinking about leaving the house (or am on my way) and I find myself wishing I was going to do something else instead – like staying at home to watch TV or browse a few websites. The second is when I am actually in the building and the service has started but I find singing the words in a heartfelt way difficult. My mind is distracted. Or simply lethargic.

This makes me feel conflicted and sometimes quite embarrassed, especially as I'm the pastor. *'I am glad they don't know that the man who is going to lead feels so ambivalent about even being there'* I think rather guiltily as I cycle to church.

One Sunday evening I thought I would begin the sermon with a confession along the lines of the previous two paragraphs. The nods of recognition and the knowing laughs around the congregation came as a bit of a relief. I discovered that (as with so many things I struggle with) my fears of being the only one like this were completely wrong. I am not alone in my own church and probably not in most others either.

Psalm 103 helps with those problems, which affect our personal prayers just as much as our difficulties with church services. In fact this psalm can really transform them. It is a piece of divinely inspired poetry which is designed to rekindle praise in our hearts. The way it works is to put words in our mouths through which we address ourselves and rouse ourselves to praise. Why not try this by saying the opening line:

| *Praise the Lord, my soul.*[1]

This is an instruction and a command to praise. We praise a person: the Lord – the one and only true God. He lives for ever and is before all time and outside all time, yet created us, revealed himself to us and relates to us as Master and Father. He is the one who deserves praise because of who he is in the incomparable greatness of his being, and because he has been so generous and kind to us in nature and in grace.

The command has a specific content: 'praise his *holy name*' (verse 1, my italics). Immediately we are into an area which is rarified: holiness. Our God is different. He has no dark corners or flaws. He simply is pure and upright. So biblical praise is about recognising his reality – as opposed to singing doubtfully about a God we aren't sure about. It is about specific recognition of his specific identity – as opposed to a God we are vague about or have decided must be like this or that according to our own personal preferences. It is about awe for his holiness, his unlikeness to us in so many ways.

But the command to self is not enough. The psalmist repeats it in the next line: 'Praise the Lord, my soul' (verse 2). The self is examined; it is not praising God. The self is diagnosed: it needs impetus. The self realises that he is the one to give this to himself so the self is directed.

The old Bible commentator Matthew Henry says:

David is talking to himself and he is no fool that thus talks to himself and excites his own soul to that which is good.[2]

I wonder if in Matthew Henry's day talking to yourself was said to be a sign of madness as it is often in ours. Perhaps that is part of the background to his saying, 'he is no fool that thus talks to himself'. Or perhaps it is a way of saying, 'It is a mark of great wisdom to talk like this to yourself.' But we shouldn't get too caught up with those relatively minor considerations. The gold here is in the last phrase: 'he is no fool that … excites his own soul to that which is good.'

Do you need to reignite the fires of praise and rekindle the glow of worship? Our fires go out or burn low. Our enthusiasm dims. And it doesn't naturally come welling up from within. But we can do something about this. We are not stuck in the mediocrity of half-heartedness. We can rouse ourselves. David invites us to engage in an inner dialogue in which we use our mind and our memory to rouse our emotions.

In all areas of life we can get used to having something – perhaps a pay rise or the return to health after an injury or an illness – and start to take it for granted. Thomas Hardy, the well-known novelist, also wrote poetry. (Some people think his poems are better than his novels.) His *Poems of 1912–13* were written after his wife, Emma, died. Their marriage had failed to excite Hardy very much for years. Then she died. And only then did he realise how much he had loved her.

The poems express the loss of what he hadn't appreciated at the time.

We can stop appreciating the Lord. We can forget all the good things he has done for us. That must have been true for David because he says rather firmly to himself:

Praise the Lord, my soul,
*   and forget not all his benefits (Psalm 103:2).*

This kind of inner self-talk is precisely what many of us need. Our problem is not that we don't have an inner dialogue; it's that we have a different one going on in which we listen to ourselves instead of talking to ourselves.[3] The inner feelings and thoughts we listen to are the ones that stop praise coming. If we just pay attention to them, we will very often find an excuse not to go to church – or when we get there, will take part in a detached way. It may well mean we spend our time at church critical of others (or perhaps ourselves). And then we fail to praise God as we might. In any situation there is always something for a Christian to praise God.

Of course there are times when this is harder than ever to do. My father died on Christmas Eve a few years ago and I was quite subdued in the service on Christmas Day. But God still enabled me to sing praise to Christ with authenticity – my dad's death was sad but God was still God and worthy of praise. In those situations it is amazing how the right kind of gospel self-talk enables praise.

When you don't feel like coming to church, could you talk to yourself this way? Or when you are at church and a hymn is announced but you don't feel very much inside, could you talk to yourself this way? Do so using the words of Psalm 103. This is the genius of the psalm: all you have to do is read it out loud. But as you read it, you will find yourself talking to yourself. It will put words into your mouth which, as you say them, cause something to happen: gospel self-talk!

Here's an experiment you might want to try. Why not read Psalm 103 out loud on your own every day this week? It doesn't take very long. The last time I tried was one afternoon when I was probably a bit sleepy. It took me 1 minute 45 seconds. So if you could find 2 minutes in your daily schedule, I invite you to try this – and to savour the benefits. If you think two minutes is too long, how about just the first five verses? That takes no more than a few seconds! As you do, you'll be drawn into practising biblical self-talk about dryness in worship. I am confident that your worship will therefore be different.

David not only starts Psalm 103 with 'Praise the Lord, my soul'; he ends on the same note. This is the beginning, not the end, of praise which is never-ending. As Matthew Henry puts it:

> *When we have done ever so much in the service of God, yet still we must stir ourselves up to do more. God's praise is a subject that will never be exhausted, and therefore we must never think that this work is done till we come to heaven when it will be forever.*[4]

Questions

What do you think of the idea of learning biblical self-talk to overcome problems with praise? Is it something you might benefit from? Are you listening to yourself rather than talking to yourself?

SELF-TALK'S TWO FORMATS

Version one – listening to self

This is an inner dialogue of the kind we tend to have without always vocalising it:

I really don't feel like a quiet time.

You poor thing, tell me why?

I'm really tired.

Bad night?

And some.

[silence]

And I had one yesterday and the day before.

Gosh, that's good going.

And I don't want to get legalistic.

Absolutely not – avoid that like the plague.

And there's just too much to do today.

Like what?

Got to have a shower and wash my hair; get an online shop done so it comes after work; and do some admin – bills, emails and stuff. Then it's a normal work day but I'm seeing Judy for lunch (and that's going to take loads out of me). Then I've Bible study this evening and then my mother needs a call …

You're really overloaded. Best give it a miss?

Version two – talking to self

This is an inner dialogue where we choose to use words to talk to ourselves!

I really don't feel like a quiet time.

Not nice but how much do feelings come into it?

Well, I'm tired and really busy.

OK but does that make some sort of quiet time more or less of a good idea?

God can get by without me, can't he?

That's not really the point, is it?

What do you mean?

Surely the main point is that God is great and simply deserves your praise?

I know, I know.

And even if he can get along without you, can you really get along without him on such a busy day when you're feeling wrung out?

Well …

[interrupting] I mean surely this is the sort of situation when what you need most of all is to remind yourself how great God is …

Yes but …

[interrupting again] and tell him how much you need him so you can cope with Judy at lunchtime without getting fed up with her.

OK but I really can't spend ages working out all the words in my Bible text and praying halfway through the house group email prayer update.

Sure. It may not be the day for that. But what about saying Psalm 103:1–2 to yourself, reading your Bible chapter thoughtfully, saying the Lord's Prayer meaningfully and then asking for help for today's pinch points?

OK.

4

When I feel too rubbish for God

Here is a part-imagined, part-real conversation with a friend:

How're things? I'm feeling unbearably irritable with any human being I meet. Sometimes it's the near to unbearable weight of just being me.

Oh brother, I'm so sorry. I know it well. I call those my hate-the-world days. Had one yesterday.

Thanks. That helps. I wish I loved the human race. I wish I loved its stupid face. I wish I loved the way it walks. I wish I loved the way it talks. And when I'm introduced to one, I wish I thought: 'What jolly fun.' But what do I do?

Have you tried talking to God about it?

He's the last person I feel I can go to.

Why?

Because I am so horrible.

And?

I don't want him to see how horrible I am.

Is that logical?

What do you mean?

If he's God, he can see it already.

Yeah, I know. But I can't see him seeing me. Whereas if I start praying about how I feel, then I will be more aware of it and I'll feel worse.

Have you tried the prayer of self-surrender?[1]

Is this more of that trendy stuff?

Trendy? Me?

Ha. Go on then.

There's a lot in the Bible about offering ourselves to God. Paul says we should offer our bodies as living sacrifices in Romans 12:1. A bit earlier, in Romans 6:15–23, he talks about offering every part of ourselves as instruments of righteousness.

That's exactly the problem. I'm not an instrument of righteous tunes; I am an instrument badly out of tune. It feels as though I have notes too high and low for the human ear which are uglier still.

Do you want to give this a go or not?

OK. What do I do then?

Find a place to be quiet. Ideally this would be a physical place but you may need to make a quiet space inside your mind.

Right, I'm on my own and the radio is off.

And your phone! Now sit (or lie) quietly and open yourself to God's eyes.

How?

Look at him as you look deep inside yourself. Be attentive to the rubbish you find. Go beneath what you wish you were. Go down to what you are worried about. Pay attention to the things about you (or your life) that are disappointing. Or that make you feel ashamed.

Yup. There's quite a lot there.

Make sure you are moving towards God, or allowing yourself to be aware that he is looking at you. Tell him that you are not what you want to be or should be, and that you know that.

OK. Feels like a start.

You may want to go deeper still.

Why?

Because none of us really knows or understands ourselves. We just can't. It's partly because we are finite beings with finite knowledge. We have deeper inner capacities than we have the ability to know. So it is like a dog trying to understand how a television works.

Gosh.

It's also because we have all sorts of inner cloaking devices that hide our true selves from ourselves.

Like defence mechanisms – denial and so on?

Exactly. Freud got that spot on.

Good old Lucien.

Sigmund!

So what do I do?

How do you feel about not knowing all that is going on deep inside you that produces your excessive anxiety, your overwork?

Embarrassed. Frustrated. Annoyed.

OK. Now move towards God, realising – and this is really important – that he knows you perfectly.

I find it hard to make that move.

Look at the cross. Remember God's promise to put us right with him through Jesus.

OK, I'm trying.

How does that feel?

We may be getting somewhere.

Move towards him in faith, bringing all that you are and surrendering yourself to him for help because you cannot help yourself and you have nowhere else to go.

I could have a drink or eat some chocolate.

Will they really help?

Nope. I could look at some porn.

Oh yeah?

I know that would be sinful. I could watch a box set. I've this new one I've almost finished.

Sounds like that will really deal with your problems …

OK, I could … if I could just pick up my phone and …

Hah! And what? Did your phone die for you? Is God on Facebook or Instagram?

But my phone, well, it's just …

Yes?

It's what I turn to when I feel lousy or bored or fed up. It's what I was doing when I saw you were online – so there you go!

Yes, but we are talking on your landline now – and your phone is in the next room.

I have nowhere else to go but God.

So why not talk to him?

What, over the phone?

Well, I'm happy to listen and help if you want.

Definitely. OK, here goes:

Lord, it's not great that I am coming to you as my last resort but that's what you are here. Even that makes me realise how messed up I am inside and how little I really get myself.

Why have I been so horrible to people in the last 24 hours? Why have I had such critical reactions to people who were just trying their best? I really don't want to be like this but something deep inside – that is me but isn't me – seems to take over.

That's a great start.

And I compare it with who I like to think I am and the difference is awful.

Keep going.

O Lord, you do know me completely. Better than I know myself … but this is pretty embarrassing …

Now is the moment to remember the cross. Bring it to mind. Glue yourself to it. Remember it was for you. All your shameful stuff. Your whole inner, messed-up, dark being. Even the nice you that you have tried to create to be proud of. It's all nailed there. Finito! Gone. Dealt with. Over.

Lord, really? Why? How?

Good questions. But now think of the father of the prodigal son and his open arms.

Lord, I give myself back to you. Thank you that all my stinking, twisted stuff is nailed on the cross. Thank you that you're doing this now.

Move towards those arms by faith. Make the move inside. Give yourself wholly to him.

Why 'wholly'?

You aren't just going for a spiritual and emotional bath so you can get on with life again.

How did you know I was half thinking that?

Because it's what I do! Moving towards God means giving him all you can of yourself at that moment. The horrible stuff to forgive and put right. The half good stuff to be purged of pride and be improved. The plans you have for big and little things to be given over to him. It's surrender, submission, abandoning yourself to him.

It feels like part of me is resisting that.

Yup, that's normal.

So what do I do?

Do you want to give yourself to him unconditionally?

Yes – I just feel resistance within.

Good, that's normal.

So …

Tell him. Tell him what you want but what you find hard. Then give yourself to him.

I sort of get what you mean but …

I know, it is always complicated and a bit messy – I think it always will be. The idea that it is a simple move is a bit naive. But it is still a move we can and must make.

So I just have to do it?

More or less. Why not do whatever you can right now?

Lord, I want to want you. I want to want to give myself entirely to you. I am over halfway there – maybe 85% actually – but the last 15% is really hard. But here's how I am. Take me. As much as I can at this moment, I hand myself over to you. It's your life, not mine. It's your body, not mine. It's your future, not mine. It's your stuff, not mine. The 15% is banging away inside trying to derail this but I am sticking with you. I want you. I want you more than anything else. I want to be yours more than anything else. Amen.

So how do you feel now?

Different! Better. Safe. Loved. Realigned somehow. Or do I mean reoriented? Something different is in the middle of me – Christ, I guess.

And all those negative critical thoughts?

In the past. And irrelevant in the present. Because Jesus has come home.

What this dialogue illustrates is the way we wind ourselves into knots with our own sense of failure. It is true that we fail. We know that. But Christ never wants us to get stuck in the superglue of our own mistakes. He wants to draw near. He wants to lift us up. He wants to show us his love and his work, done once for all on the cross. Whatever state we are in or feel we are in, he wants us near him.

Questions

Where did you see yourself in the long dialogue? Which parts of the helpful friend's words helped you?

Prayer

Lord, thank you that there is no pit so deep you can't go deeper, to join me and then lift me up again. Thank you that there is no darkness so dark that your light can't shine into it with healing power. Amen.

5

When I am too frazzled to pray

A few years ago my mother and I went on a painting holiday in Andalusia, Southern Spain. We flew out to Malaga expecting to be part of a group, but when we arrived at the airport, we were the only arrivals being met by our host and teacher, Ian. The group was just us.

It could have felt a bit odd but in fact it was wonderful. Ian was a superb instructor, helping my mother develop her watercolour skills and encouraging me as I splashed away with oil paints. But Ian was more than a painting teacher; he saw himself as our host and even our holiday director.

On the first morning he had arranged to meet us at 9.30 a.m. in the hotel lobby. We bounced out of bed, had our breakfast and were waiting at 9.25 a.m., our behinds barely touching the chairs, our painting kit ready to be snatched up at a moment's notice and our muscles poised to spring into action.

'I thought we'd have a coffee before we go out,' Ian said. So we did – and drank it slowly. Or at least he drank it slowly. We waited patiently. At last his moderately sized cup was empty. We followed him out to his car and set off, slowly, along winding roads to an unknown, untouched hill town where we parked. 'At last,' we were thinking, 'a bit of painting!'

We got out of the car and walked, slowly, through the village with Ian. We passed a little café. He stopped.

'How about a coffee?' he asked. It wasn't exactly what either of us was thinking of at that moment but we were too English and inhibited to say so. All three of us sat down. Ian ordered coffees all round and proceeded to roll a cigarette. The combination of his coffee and his cigarette took some time to finish. Paying the bill took a bit longer. Ian was in no hurry. By now I was beginning to wonder if we were the victims of holiday fraud: had Ian taken our booking with no intention of any painting at all? We strolled even more slowly through the village with time to look at the crumbling butter-coloured stone, the uneven wooden doors, the bright-coloured shutters. Eventually he found the place he had earmarked. We sat down and he started us on an initial sketching exercise. In his mind we were now ready to begin.

This pattern repeated itself throughout our week with Ian. It revealed to both my mother and me just how 'task-oriented' we were. We had come on a painting holiday: we wanted to get on with being as productive with our painting as humanly possible, with no time to spare before getting our brushes out. But Ian wanted us to enjoy Andalusia: the coffee, the warmth, the ageing stone, the ochre and olive pastel shades of the parched mountain sides. Ian had worked out that if we relaxed, slowed down, noticed what was all around us and so on, then we were likely to paint better too!

That movement towards stillness is one that most people know (I include myself) would benefit from making more often in their lives. And so would most of the Christians I know (as I have myself and continue to need). How can we do that?

It is not a matter of praying more. Prayer can be as busy and task-oriented as washing up the coffee cups after church. (Though, oddly enough, washing up can be a special time of resting in the presence of God. Doubtful? Read on!)

We tend to think of stillness as God's gift to us:

He makes me lie down in green pastures.
He leads me beside still *waters (Psalm 23:2,* esv, *my emphasis).*

That is the good shepherd at work. He leads; we follow. But, as is the case so often, there is another side to it. Christians frequently quote Psalm 46:10:

He says, 'Be still, *and know that I am God;*
I will be exalted among the nations,
I will be exalted in the earth' (My emphasis).

Sometimes other Christians point out that God is talking here to a nation at war rather than Christians in an agitated state. But we should not leave it there because other verses speak of a practice of 'self-stilling'. Here is one:

Be still *before the Lord*
and wait patiently for him;
do not fret when people succeed in their ways,
when they carry out their wicked schemes (Psalm 37:7, my emphasis).

Notice the command is to be still before the Lord. It's

an invitation but a bit more too: it's a command to someone who has got all agitated about successful people whose wealth is built on the pain of others; a failure of social and economic justice; a world which seems morally topsy-turvy. It could also apply to any kind of personal agitation.

It was written by David, perhaps because he had found that he needed to still himself – and had learned how to do that, as we see in Psalm 131. There is nothing quite like it anywhere else in the Bible – a poem in which someone describes his movement towards God. It is also addressed to God; it is a prayer. The prayer of Psalm 131 starts with a statement that startles:

My heart is not proud, LORD,
my eyes are not haughty.

I wonder if you have ever prayed like that? I don't think I have – and if I have, I would worry that it would make me like the Pharisee in Jesus' parable who thanked God that he was better than other people (Luke 18:11). If I was going to get really complicated, I would worry that by praying like this I would be in danger of being proud of not being proud!

But David does say these words and he doesn't seem to make it as complicated as I would. In fact it's the opposite: the whole thing is a movement away from that sort of complication. For this great king calming himself is not a matter of getting his breathing right or having a break from royal duties. It is an inner movement away from one thing and into something else. He chooses to switch focus:

I do not concern myself with great matters
or things too wonderful for me (Psalm 131:1).

David moves away from aspiring to be God. We all do that, from kings to coal miners. Each of us overreaches in what we think it is our business to know and to worry about. So often that is what keeps us from praying. We are absorbed with anxiety and concern. Prayer feels like a luxury we can't afford or a resource that might just possibly help us as we carry the cares of the universe on our shoulders. But God does not want us to treat him as dispensable or useful. He wants us to treat him like a mother.

For that to be true in David's life he had to set aside the things that were God's concern not his. So do we. When David did this, he discovered:

I have calmed and quietened myself (Psalm 131:2).

There is a deliberate calming and quietening of the inner self. Too often I think this is something God should be doing to me. It is his work of course: he makes me lie down by still waters. But I have my own role too – that is the whole point of what David is saying. He is the subject of the sentence, the person who does something. For him that means intentionally switching off from trying to be god-like and settling into being childlike:

I am like a weaned child with its mother (Psalm 131:2).

There is nothing childish about this. Actually the childish thing is wanting to be god-like! King David, a mature man and believer, chooses to see himself as a little child snuggled up with his mother. I've puzzled over the phrase 'weaned child'. My best shot at understanding it is that this is different from a breast-feeding child who needs his mother to pick him up and put him on the breast. There is a bit more independent choice here. An older child does more for themselves but still on occasion snuggles back with their mother to feel loved and safe. The result is very ordinary and highly desirable:

... like a weaned child I am content (Psalm 131:2).

David does not experience a dramatic result, like fireworks, but the onset of a calm peace. Other concerns have passed away. In the presence of God there is safety, acceptance and contentment. It is so wonderful for David that he recommends it to others, including us:

Israel, put your hope in the LORD
    both now and for evermore (Psalm 131:3).

This is not a private privilege for us to envy but an open invitation for us to accept. We know God as our Father but in this psalm he shows us that he is also *like* the very best of mothers.[1]

Questions

What would it look like for you to 'slow down'? What could you change to make that possible? How could you follow David's pattern?

Prayer

Lord, I am not at all sure how I can take the initiative in this as David did. It feels a bit as though either you are going to have to do it for me or it won't happen. But I really like what this psalm teaches me and I want to do this. Thank you that the psalm is your invitation to me to do the same. Please help me. Amen.

6

When God seems invisible and distant

Abraham Kuyper was born in Holland in 1837. He became a pastor but wasn't yet a real believer. This very bright young man then learned the gospel from his much less educated parishioners and became a Christian. Over time he did advanced theological study to become a theologian but branched out, being elected as a member of the Dutch Parliament. He went on to found a newspaper and a trade union, while his career in public life culminated in a term as Prime Minister of the Netherlands from 1901 to 1905. He was one of the highest achieving Christian activists of all time.

What is not well known is that Kuyper wrote a devotional meditation every week for 40 years of his life, writing 2000 in all. One hundred and ten of them are collected in his book *To Be Near unto God* and they all explore, with some creativity, this one part of Psalm 73:28: 'it is good for me to draw near to God' (av).[1] I wonder how that thought impacts your prayer life?

God is present everywhere. Theologians call this his 'omnipresence'. 'Omni' comes from the Latin word for 'all'. God is in all places without exception. The Bible writers speak of his being everywhere to emphasise that we cannot find anywhere to hide away from him as well as to show yet another aspect of how immeasurably great he is. He fills the entire universe without that exhausting his being. If (and it is a big if) there are multiple universes, he fills every one of them – and that is a drop in the ocean of his immensity. That means that we do not have to go on long journeys or pilgrimages to try to find the place where God lives.

God is everywhere but specially present to people who have become Christians. Through Christ we have been authorised and invited into the very presence of God, something that would previously have been unthinkable, impossible and dangerous because of our sin. This is the great and main point of Hebrews 4 – 10, culminating in:

> *Therefore, brothers and sisters, since we have confidence to enter the Most Holy Place by the blood of Jesus, by a new and living way opened for us through the curtain, that is, his body, and since we have a great priest over the house of God,* let us draw near to God *with a sincere heart and with the full assurance that faith brings, having our hearts sprinkled to cleanse us from a guilty conscience and having our bodies washed with pure water* (Hebrews 10:19-22, my emphasis).

God is everywhere and he is specially present and accessible to Christians but we need to realise that and draw near to him. The writer of Hebrews says there is something for us to do.

Imagine a school teacher. On the third day of the autumn term her new class are unruly. Her presence in that classroom will be firm, authoritative, even a bit severe if that is needed. A few weeks later one of her students approaches her hesitantly at the end of a lesson. As she starts to speak, she becomes tearful. The teacher uses all her empathy to draw the girl out. She explains that her mum has been in hospital since the summer and things are difficult at home. The way the teacher is 'present' to the girl will be very different.

That evening the teacher arrives home and, without stopping to sit down, starts cooking dinner for her family for the agreed time of 6.30 p.m. At 7.15 p.m. her 15-year-old son saunters in, without explanation or apology, and wolfs down his food, while updating his status on Facebook and muttering about dinner being cold. The following evening the teacher goes out to a concert. A friend of hers is playing in the orchestra. She sits very still, completely quiet and full of attention to the music.

These varying scenarios show that there are several different ways in which different people are aware that she is 'present'. Likewise our perception of God's presence can vary hugely, even if he is always 'there'. Therefore so many biblical writers encourage us consciously to draw near to him, to realise that he is near, to be attentive to his presence.

I realise I am trying to describe what is indescribable and also very personal. But here is my current best effort to put my understanding of drawing near to God into words:

- It is a conscious inner movement of faith towards the God who has never gone away but whose presence we have forgotten.

- It is an intentional choice in which we move ourselves towards God on the basis of his invitation to come to him. We feel our sin but our sin drives us to our Saviour in repentance and faith. We feel our pain but our pain drives us to our Healer in expectation and faith.

• It is an internal movement of faith-driven imagination.

By 'imagination' I do not mean either something we invent like an imaginary friend or something that is untrue. What we imagine can be something made up or manufactured. You can try to imagine that you are sitting on a beach but you aren't – you are on a chair or sofa.

Imagination in the sense I mean is that inner part of us which can conceptualise and picture and be gripped by a reality that is not always so clear to us. Imagine you know you are going on holiday to a familiar beach. Most of the time you don't think about the beach but sometimes you do – your imagination brings it to mind. Then you move towards it in your inner being as you remember being there and think about again experiencing the sea breezes and the smell of the seaweed. It is something truly beautiful and exciting (or something dull or frightening too).

So it is not fake or false to think about moving close to God. It is using the faculty of imagination with the help of the Holy Spirit to bring to mind what is real: that we have access to God through Christ; that he is actually near to us; that he is a constant, strong, faithful presence. It is grasping hold by faith of something that is real but unseen.
One writer has described it as being like:

... stretching out your hand towards a mirror and discovering

that the mirror isn't a hard surface but a liquid one; a kind of porous, reflective, liquid membrane that you can pass your hand through to an unseen reality the other side. The membrane is wafer thin but it is reflective and looks solid. The devil tells us it is impermeable; the devil tells us that there is nothing on the other side. But those are lies. Our natural minds tell us that it is impermeable and there is nothing there. But the eyes of our hearts move beyond our natural minds. By faith we can penetrate to the other side into the reality of God's presence. We step by faith into his presence and we find ourselves breathing new air.[2]

That has an effect. When there is someone else in the room, how I feel is different. I am aware of them: of who they are, of what they are like, of what I am in relation to them. If Jesus was physically in the room, the same would be true.

Drawing near to God has those sorts of effects on us. There may be unconfessed sin which makes us feel guilty and so we confess it and get right with God. It may make us realise things we need to do differently, a bit like having the boss walking into the room or the captain coming onto the deck.

But for Christians struggling on in faith, the effects of drawing near to God are overwhelmingly positive – we feel the reality of his love; we feel the security of resting our lives in his hands. Our perspective is changed and transformed by the felt reminder that God is real and dominant and good – and for us. We feel what it means when God said we are forgiven and that he has made us his children. And we feel what it means to move towards a father who is welcoming us. Our souls are put at rest. Things are put back in perspective.

This is a movement behind the curtain into the inner holy of holies, to use the Old Testament temple imagery of Hebrews 6:19. As we make this movement of faith, we find the hope that Jesus gives us and this becomes the anchor of our souls, with firmness and security.

Abraham Kuyper wrote about the twin dangers of a dry proposition-based orthodoxy and also of what he called a 'sickly mysticism', by which he meant a sentimental, undemanding, wishy-washy, low-octane, fat-free version of a relationship with God. What sustained him was this sense of the presence of the living God in all his transcendent majesty and his holy weight. He kept working for God right to the end of his life, nurtured by this inner walk with the Lord. But in time his strength waned. A colleague came to see him. It was clear that Kuyper was dying so he asked him a question: 'Shall I tell the people that God has been your refuge and strength to the end?' Kuyper could only manage a weak reply, hardly more than a whisper, but it was very clear: 'Yes, altogether!'

Imagine walking into a room which is a bit darker than outside and then sitting down. Your eyes take a while to adjust to the lower light. You assume that you are on your own. As your eyes become accustomed to the low light, you become aware that there is someone else in the room actually sitting quite close to you. For a moment you are a little startled but then you see that they are smiling at you. You have a powerful sense of being loved and that you are safe there.[3] That can be more of your daily experience with God – a growing consciousness of what is real; the close presence of infinite love and greatness to hold and keep you.

Questions

Think for a moment about how much you draw near to God or simply realise his presence close to you. Do you sense his invitation for that to happen more often?

Prayer

Lord, I long to know your presence more. Help me to respond to your invitation to come. Amen.

7

When sadness or anger get in the way

Often we struggle to pray because we are just feeling low about something – or everything – and think we have to be happy to pray. That's not so according to the Bible. If your problem is thinking this way, there is a happy surprise for you here.

I preached a sermon with the title 'If you aren't groaning, you should be!' It was intended to startle people – and then to help them. As the apostle Paul writes:

We know that the whole creation has been groaning as in the pains of childbirth right up to the present time (Romans 8:22).

Muzak is that kind of background music that plays in lifts. It drives sensitive musicians (and others) mad because of its banality. But there is a kind of background music in our world that is far from banal: the sad song of creation. This is a song without words but with deep feeling because this world is not as it should be, and getting to where it should be in Christ is excruciatingly painful. Creation is like a woman in childbirth and the groans of childbirth can be extraordinary. I heard of two women in labour who could hear each other through the walls of the maternity unit; enough said.

Creation's background music is also the background music of our hearts:

Not only so, but we ourselves, who have the firstfruits of the Spirit, groan inwardly as we wait eagerly for our adoption to sonship, the redemption of our bodies. For in this hope we were saved. But hope that is seen is no hope at all. Who hopes for what they already have? But if we hope for what we do not yet have, we wait for it patiently (Romans 8:23–25).

We are waiting for our glorious future but as we wait we groan. We groan because of what we have – the down payment of the Spirit. We thought earlier about the amazing presence of the Holy Spirit in our hearts who makes real to us that Jesus is our brother and has made God our Father. Every time we say 'Father' to God, that is the Holy Spirit speaking. We live supernaturalised lives.

Here is another side to it: the very presence of the Spirit reminds us how far there is to go. It reminds us of our remaining sin, which puzzles us and plagues us. The little tastes of heaven that he gives us make the sourness of this life feel all the more intolerable. The hope of bodies and souls put right in heaven makes us realise how much pain there is in life now. And as we look outside of our world, we groan with friends who are ill or troubled. We groan at a world with so much that needs putting right and apparently no one able to put it right.

So we groan because of what we have and because of what we don't have. That is a type of praying – and one that comes from the Spirit:

In the same way, the Spirit helps us in our weakness. We do not know what we ought to pray for, but the Spirit himself intercedes for us through wordless groans (Romans 8:26).

I take the view that the Spirit's 'wordless groans' are our wordless groans, just as he is the one who is speaking as we say 'Abba Father' to God. So, again, to be a Christian is to live a supernaturalised life.

Graham Beynon produced a nice book on emotions which included this:

> *… we must beware the caricature of the happy smiling Christian. To be honest I don't trust a happy smiling Christian – something is usually being covered up. We will feel a whole variety of emotions, including 'negative' ones. Those negative emotions, felt for good reason, are right, normal, expected, godly.[1]*

Why is this in a book on prayer? Because biblically this is a part of prayer. Large numbers of the psalms are groans. The book of Lamentations is a bleak, five-part groan about the ruins of Jerusalem. The Holy Spirit puts groans in our hearts: we need to recognise them as prayers and go with the flow.

But we need to be careful that our groaning is not grumbling. That is different, largely because it has lost sight of what is coming. People without a future hope do grumble-groans:

> *One of the saddest things is to know someone who is suffering in this present who has only that present. What pessimism it has produced; what grim despair! It is summed up in Benjamin*

D'Israeli's aphorism: 'Youth is a blunder; manhood a struggle; old age a regret', and by Thomas Hardy: 'All is trouble, adversity and suffering.'[2]

The Bible steers us rather firmly away from that. But as it does so, it steers us firmly towards the right sort of negative rumbling:

Learning to groan is a key aspect of the Christian response to problems. The Bible gives us permission to express our pain. We find that over one-third of the psalms are laments where God's faithful servants groan about their problems.[3]

The psalms can be the best way to do this verbally, when wordless groans are not enough. But whether we groan with or without words, we must realise that this is God at work in us and he is listening to us. We are experiencing:

... a groaning which is the breathing of life not throb of death. The deep groanings of the heart are the muffled chimings of heaven.[4]

When the only prayer you can manage is a groan, that is a beautiful prayer in the sight of God.[5]

God not only hears our groanings but he understands them.[6]

Nor are these truths just about us and our own pains; this is true for the whole human race in all its muddle and pain. I have grown to love the song 'Mothers of the Disappeared' by U2. It goes back to the 1980s when death squads operated in several countries in Central and South America with impunity, kidnapping and killing many people who they felt were undesirable or threatening. The song speaks in the voice of the mothers whose children have been taken. Singing, humming or listening to it can be a sort of groaning in the Spirit:

> In the trees our sons stand naked
> Through the walls our daughters cry
> See their tears in the rainfall.[7]

That is a lament; a groan. God wants to hear our groans! If we turn them towards him, we are praying in the power of the Holy Spirit.

Why not make that more specific? News media tends to feature stories which are shocking or alarming. That is probably the nature of the medium and not something that is likely to change. The big question for believers is what we do with the groans we feel at these stories of injustice and suffering. (If we don't feel groans, then we ought to ask the Holy Spirit to work deep within us). The Bible's answer is that groaning leads onto intercession, crying out to God for his action against suffering and injustice. That does not have to be a complicated kind of prayer! It is a prayer for God to bring relief. Paul also encourages us to pray for those in authority to exercise their power well (1 Timothy 2:1–3) as that is surely a key part of such praying.

Note though that sometimes people pray about injustice

as though we can expect universal peace before Jesus returns. That is not the biblical view. Equally sometimes people forget that God works through wars and social breakdown to bring people to eternal salvation. The whole of Isaiah shows how this works. It is good to pray as much if not more for conversions of eternal significance in war zones as it is to pray for peace which is only ever relative and partial.

Questions

How has this chapter impacted your view of your groans? If you can see that you grumble rather than groan, how can you move from one to the other? And then move onto asking God to work on the problems that make you groan?

Prayer

Lord, there is so much that seems rubbish. And it hurts. Help. And please do something. Amen.

8

When asking for things seems silly

At last we are at what many people think of as the essence of prayer: asking God to do things! And that is entirely right. He tells us to relate to him as our heavenly Father. How do children relate to their earthly fathers? They ask them for things! Star Wars Lego for Christmas; help with maths homework; tomato ketchup with fish fingers; a second bedtime story. Fathers of older children get used to a special tone, 'Da-ad ...?' to which the answer is: 'How much, darling?'

Our heavenly Father expects, commands and wants us to ask him to do things for us and for others. In the Lord's Prayer we say, 'Give us this day our daily bread', which is a shorthand or catch-all for all we need today to make life continue. It expresses our dependence, reminds us that we are not self-sufficient and most of all declares, 'Lord, I need you and your help to get through today!'

People call these kinds of prayers *supplication* (when asking for things for ourselves) and *intercession* (when asking for things for other people). Both are right. Neither is better or worse than the other. Neither should be abandoned in favour of the other. Jesus did both and so should we!

Here is another imaginary dialogue between a younger and an older Christian about what asking God for things looks like in practice:

So how do I pray for myself? What can I ask for?

What will enable you to fulfil God's will in your life.

That's easy to say! But what is that?

It's what the Bible says is his will: food, protection, money, work, a home, relationships of different kinds.

Is that all in the Bible?

Sure. God's will is for us to be relational not solitary creatures. So to have different kinds of relationships and – for many but not all people – to marry and have children.

So I can pray about that?

You should!

Surely I can't pray about money?

God says we should provide for ourselves (and any dependents) and also give money to the poor and to support Christian workers. How can you do that without money? Why would you not pray about it?

Well, it seems a bit unspiritual.

I know. But when you think about it, which is less spiritual: praying about money or not praying about money?

Ha! Got me there, I suppose. And you are going to say the same applies to jobs and houses and everything else?

Absolutely. Don't forget 1 Timothy 4:4–5: '... everything God created is good, and nothing is to be rejected if it is received with thanksgiving, because it is consecrated by the word of

God and prayer.'

How does that help?

God wants to give us good things. And he wants us to receive them thankfully as things that are set apart for his service. We are to use them according to what the Bible teaches and with prayer. So praying about money, possessions and all the good things of this world is commanded!

Yeah, but how do I do that without it feeling as though I am sending an Internet shopping order to someone I expect to deliver on time and totally as I ask?

Great, great question. The key thing is what Jesus said in the garden.

Of Gethsemane?

Yes: 'not my will, but yours be done'. Or as we should put it: 'if it is your will'.

So I just say 'if it is your will' every time and I will receive what I want?

No. That makes it a formula and relationships don't work by formulae.

So do I say it or not?

You mean it as you ask.

What?

You let your inclinations focus on a legitimate and possible job or house (or future spouse even) and express those desires to

God. But you work at the same time at being willing for him to work out whether those things are for you now or ever.

That sounds a bit hard.

A bit. But biblical and worth it.

Give me an example.

OK. Imagine someone with a little investment in an Internet start-up that could produce either a lot of money or just a bit. That person imagines being more financially independent in the future and maybe even having more money to give away to others. Both seem like good things so she asks God to make the start-up go well. But at the same time she becomes very aware that she is thinking about money too much so she repents of that. And she is also aware that God might have a better plan for her than having lots more money ...

Sorry? A better plan than lots more money?

Oh yes. Money could ruin her life spiritually and relationally. She is aware of that. So while she prays for it to succeed, she keeps saying, 'If that is what you want and what is best for me.' And when she feels she wants it too much, she turns back towards the greater treasure there is in Christ. She has been fantasising about a special house next to a river but turns those longings towards Jesus like this:

> You are all sweetness to me
> You are lawns rolling down to the river
> You are stately wellingtonia trees

> You are the meadows beyond the light on the water
> The most delicate morning mist
> The rose-red ripples of sunset
> You are the party in the barn
> The quiet rest time from the bedroom with a view
> You are all this and far more.

That feels a bit of a long answer to a question you may or may not have been asking so let's get back to asking prayers. The takeaway point is: ask God for the things you think you need. Keep asking him. And pray for other people as well.

How? Who?

Pray for those you love. For your nearest and dearest. Most people make them a priority and rightly so.

But how?

I'd suggest praying for their wellbeing in every way, but especially spiritually. Let the kinds of prayers you find in Scripture guide you. Generally speaking what Paul prays for more than anything is deeper knowledge of God, more holiness, more love, more faith, more hope. Health definitely comes into it but the emphasis is more on spiritual health than physical healing. (I know which I would rather have even if I'd like both ideally.)

What about other people?

Yes, yes, yes. Only praying for family and close friends isn't very Christian! We all have circles of connection and need.

Out of Christian love we should pray for these people.

For what exactly?

The same as for family: general and specific needs, both practical and spiritual, but with the emphasis on the spiritual – knowing Christ more above all.

How do you even start organising all that?

Most people need lists. Some people seem to have very effective prayer lives without lists but I think they are the exception not the rule.

How do I make a list?

Well it's up to you but here is one way to start. Why not work out a little pattern like this:

1. People you pray for every day.
2. People you pray for once a week – having a list so that you know who you pray for each day.
3. People who you pray for on a longer rotating basis – perhaps using missionary prayer letters or other prayer guides.

Sounds a bit complicated.

Not really. You can put that on a single small card to keep in your Bible or by your bed. Over time you can adapt it, adding names or perhaps taking some away. If your experience is anything like mine, God will develop it gradually.

But I do everything on my smartphone! Ha! You hadn't thought of that, had you?

Well I'm stuck on paper but actually I have a lot of friends who use their phones to read the Bible and to organise their prayers. I've heard people lifting the roof with their praises of an app called PrayerMate.[1]

Bet it's expensive.

Actually it's free.

Bet it's complicated.

They say it's really easy and it gives you very helpful reminders so you don't forget to pray for people.

I'm almost persuaded.

Good. And there's another dimension to intercession that we really ought to mention.

Go on.

Praying for the spread of the gospel at home and abroad. This is so easy to forget when we are already trying to remember to move closer to God, calm ourselves in his presence, stir ourselves up to praise him, and pray for ourselves and our friends. But it really matters. Paul continually asks people to pray for him to have courage to tell people about Jesus and for fruit to come from this.

It sounds a bit advanced.

Not at all. It is for everyone. Start small.

Give me an example.

Try praying once a week for people to become Christians

through your church.

And if they don't?

Pray a bit more often and a bit more specifically. Perhaps pray for the mums and toddlers group on Tuesdays and the Youth Group on Fridays. Pray for your pastor or vicar on Saturday evenings as they prepare to preach on Sundays.

And if I still don't see conversions?

Keep praying. I have one friend who prayed for his best friend every day for 18 months. As he was only around 19 himself, that seemed like a huge stretch of time. But he kept praying and his friend did become a Christian. I know a mother whose son lost interest in church aged 13 and stopped coming but she never stopped praying and never gave up. She kept imagining his baptism. He was baptised at the age of 23. I know other people who have prayed and prayed and their prayers have been answered after they died. So we should never give up.

It's hard to persevere.

Agreed! But the Holy Spirit helps us if we are willing to let him. And these prayers are not just for people close to us but for others on the front line of outreach, especially people called to evangelistic and missionary work. It's just wonderful when people pray for them regularly. Very often they can really tell the difference.

Often I just feel so sad about how godless the world is and how few Christians there are.

It is sad but first there are lots of people becoming Christians worldwide. Secondly, God really does answer our prayers. I know one pastor who has a text from Isaiah 37:21 written on the front of one of his prayer lists. It just says, 'because you have prayed ...' Originally God said that to King Hezekiah but my friend imagines how God may say that to him one day. That spurs him to pray.

But if God plans everything in advance, what's really the point?

The same God who plans everything in advance tells us to pray. He says he does things when we pray – and doesn't when we don't. It is a bit of a mystery that no one properly understands, perhaps because God is outside time. But the point is to obey him and pray! So ...

Yes?

Find some missionaries and pray for them!

Questions

Why not list the things that keep you from praying practically for yourself and others. Now look at those reasons. How sensible and substantial are they really?

Prayer

Lord, I pray but help me in my weakness in prayer. I ask but seem to do so without much faith. Do something to strengthen my sense of dependence and to prove to me that prayer makes a difference.

I ask but seem to ask rather selfishly. Help me surrender to your will and to go beyond myself and my immediate circle of loved ones. Help me to pray for others to know your help and love and salvation. Amen.

9

When Bible study seems a million miles from prayer

What does the word 'meditation' conjure up in your mind? For many people it is associated with Eastern religions, perhaps with yoga. It is about switching your mind off and entering zones of inner emptiness. Some parts of the broader Christian tradition veer towards this – I have already tried to explain the dangers of that.

In the Bible meditation is rather different. It is much busier!

Keep this Book of the Law always on your lips; meditate *on it day and night, so that you may be careful to do everything written in it. Then you will be prosperous and successful (Joshua 1:8, my emphasis).*

Blessed is the one
    who does not walk in step with the wicked
or stand in the way that sinners take
    or sit in the company of mockers,
but whose delight is in the law of the LORD,
    and who meditates *on his law day and night (Psalm 1:1–2, my emphasis).*

The word 'meditates' appears also in the next psalm, where it is translated 'plot':

Why do the nations conspire
  and the peoples plot in vain? (Psalm 2:1).

There is nothing wrong with either translation. They both say to me that this is not the sort of meditation where you switch your mind off and enter a long stream of dreamy nothing-muchness.

So our starting point for understanding biblical meditation is that it involves setting our minds to work, turning words over and over in thought, trying to understand them and how they connect with our lives. And of course we do this with biblical words, sentences, paragraphs, chapters, even books.

Biblical meditation starts with the words of the Bible. It is a part of Bible study but an aspect that often gets a bit lost or forgotten. We often read a passage and if nothing immediately jumps out at us, move on a little sadly, hoping it might be a bit different next time. Or we find something that does interest or trouble us, and we think a lot about it – if we are in a group, we talk about it – until we reach either a sense of having sorted it, or a point where we haven't but can't spend any more time on it. Lots of small-group Bible studies take a turn in this direction and never quite escape it. Over time some small groups find that they develop a habit in which their Bible studies regularly end up along these kinds of rather arid cul-de-sacs.

Biblical meditation means thinking hard about the text in front of us and interpreting it in its context – what kind of writing is it? Where does it come in the Bible.[1] *And then it requires working hard on its significance to me right now.* That is the crucial move. It is not anything as simplistic as that if God tells someone to go on a journey, I should start planning my holiday. But there will be a significance of this verse or passage for me right now.

The assumption is that I am not here by accident but that God is at work here through his Holy Spirit; that he always wants to speak to me through his word; that all of his word does speak to me one way or another; that in his planning of my life there is something I need today (or something that I might need in the future).

How might a Bible text connect with my life today?

- If it tells me about the subtlety and depth of sin in the human heart, what is going on in my heart that needs that reminder?

- If it speaks of the authority of Christ, how might I need to turn back and bow before the throne of the one who owns me as his slave?

- If it is about the Christian duty of forgiveness, do I need to be reminded of that now, or remember it for later when it may next be an issue.

In all this my assumptions must be as wide as the Bible's. So I may get a fright for a moment as I feel again how holy God is, and that may be what God wants right now. I may feel quite broken as I see how awful it is to forget him.

That too may be what he knows I need. I am not simply assuming that I will find a nice calm reassurance that all is well with my current direction and that God will make things easy in the future. I consciously let the text do its work and I spend time chewing it over and receiving it.

There are different practical techniques for doing this. I have tried to suggest one above which is more rational and linear – working hard on the original meaning of the text and then in quite a rational way seeing the connections with my life. I often do that and it serves the 'if A then B and so C' way of thinking I use.

But people differ and not everyone works through things quite like this. Some people grasp things much more intuitively. For example, they read about the way Joseph forgave his brothers. They then see instantly and with a disturbing clarity that they have a short- or long-term grievance against a sibling that they need to forgive if they are going to be true to the Bible's great storyline of redemption.

Other people work more imaginatively. They meditate by putting themselves in the story they are reading. So they may read Luke 19's account of Jesus' encounter with Zacchaeus the tax collector and enter imaginatively into it – being in the crowd and wondering why Jesus has stopped by the tree; being rather shocked at Jesus having a meal at Zacchaeus' house; even being Zacchaeus and climbing the tree to see Jesus and then being amazed that Jesus knew his name.

Preachers often use this kind of imaginative reconstruction and it has its benefits, particularly when there are characters it is right for us to identify with. The danger is when it is done too creatively, without being controlled by the author's intention for the passage and the Bible's own overarching gospel message. So I am not sure how helpful it is for new or less well taught Christians.

Another approach is to focus in a particular way on one image or thought, spending time turning that over and over in your mind. When I preached some sermons on Isaiah, I noticed how Isaiah used different images. I spent time thinking about them and how they applied to me and my church. I would think about pictures of ruins being rebuilt and apply them directly to Christians I know. It helped me a great deal in appreciating God's work in their lives and in mine too.

An alternative method is to turn something over and over in your head with different emphases. Think about the first verse of Psalm 23:

> The LORD is my shepherd, I lack nothing.

Now try saying it emphasising the words in italics each time:

> The LORD is my shepherd, I lack nothing.
> The LORD *is* my shepherd, I lack nothing.
> The LORD is *my* shepherd, I lack nothing.
> The LORD is my *shepherd*, I lack nothing.
> The LORD is my shepherd, I lack *nothing*.

In theory the idea seems a bit wooden, but when you do it, something rather powerful unfolds. We draw out the richness of the text without in any way imposing anything on it or abusing it. And as we do this slowly and with an awareness of God, we find connections in the deepest places. Once again this may well not simply be a kind of warm affirmation. To reaffirm 'The LORD' as our shepherd puts us firmly back under his rule. That may actually be a bit uncomfortable at first as we have to surrender again all our ideas about autonomy or having him as our personal assistant.

As we use this method, we will be wanting to bring in other biblical ideas that connect with it. One very obvious one would be the way Jesus picks up this image in John 10:14–15:

> I am the good shepherd; I know my sheep and my sheep knows me
> – just as the Father knows me and I know the Father – and I lay
> down my life for the sheep.

By drawing this into our meditation, we feel all the more what it means to have Jesus as the shepherd who provides for us. This turns us to talk to him about it.

Above all, meditation enables us to have a time with God in which we let him speak to us through his word. It is our communication with him. It is, in fact, a form or a part of praying. We are not just speaking to God in the same way we might fire off an email to someone far away who may or may not reply. Nor is it us simply speaking to a God who is present and listening but entirely silent. Nor is it even our speaking to a God who is present and listening and responds with audible words. But rather God speaks to us as his Holy Spirit works though his word dynamically and situationally, personally and responsively.

Questions

When you read the Bible, do you meditate on what you have read? What would it look like for you to try this?

Prayer

Lord, I need your word as my anchor, my satnav, my energy bar. Help me meditate on it! Amen.

10

When all I do is talk

Many people find that as prayer grows it can get a bit formulaic. This chapter is to help us keep it personal. It is about learning to fix our soul's eyes on Jesus in love and wonder.

Many books on prayer advocate turning Bible reading into meditation which in turn should become what people call contemplation. There is something helpful about this, though like all structures and systems it can become too much of a thing in its own right. When that happens, God invariably makes us fed up with it, or finds some other way to dislodge us from it.

Contemplation means looking in a way that is fixed, focused and observant. It is like attentiveness but somehow it has got a bit further on. I am attentive to the river bank where I think a kingfisher may be sitting on his favourite branch and may be about to dash impossibly low across the surface of the river with a flash of electric blue that is straight from the tropics. But I contemplate the sky above with its cloud formations at tens of thousands of feet. An old married couple may contemplate by sitting quietly in their living room gently gazing at each other in gratitude for lives lived together.

The less helpful books on this tend to suggest that if you do certain things, particularly in meditation, then a contemplative state will result – and if you are lucky, that will bring you to a place of a blissfully empty mind. I think that is a double mistake – first to see contemplation as the result of a technique rather than a gift, and secondly to depersonalise it and make it into a not-very-Christian version of Eastern mysticism.

Contemplation is seeing Christ with the eyes of faith. It is having our love and hope aroused by the sight of him in personal response to his personal love for us. The classic biblical text for it is 2 Corinthians 3:18:

> ... we all, who with unveiled faces contemplate the Lord's glory, are being transformed into his image with ever-increasing glory, which comes from the Lord, who is the Spirit.

This is about Christians. The apostle Paul may say 'we all' but immediately makes clear that he means people who have had their perception 'unveiled' by the Holy Spirit as they hear the gospel. This is a distinction that book after book on contemplation shies away from but biblically it is important and non-negotiable. The other way of looking at this point is that it is for all Christians, not just a privileged few.[1]

In 2 Corinthians 3 Paul draws on a long-standing biblical idea of seeing/not seeing the Lord. In the Old Testament there is a big stress on the invisibility of God but certain folk get a glimpse of him: Moses sees his 'back' (Exodus 33:23); Isaiah sees the hem of his robe (which filled the temple, Isaiah 6:1); Ezekiel sees 'the appearance of the likeness of the glory of the Lord' (Ezekiel 1:28). In the New Testament we find Jesus coming as 'the image of the invisible God' (Colossians

1:15) and therefore being seen by Christians of that time. For us we see by faith, not sight (1 Peter 1:8) but it is still real.

Paul picks up on this idea, using the word 'contemplation' to describe what is happening. It means gazing with a kind of quiet, fixed attention on Christ. The original Greek word refers to seeing in a mirror; as ancient mirrors were a bit blurry, this is not the face-to-face seeing of heaven. Nor is it about thinking up a possible face for Jesus and thinking about that. It is not seeing in the literal sense – for that we have to wait until heaven. But it is bringing to mind something of what we know of Jesus and fixing the thoughts of our minds upon it. This is done not so much analytically as adoringly, and with praise, letting the Holy Spirit do something deep and transforming in us as we do.

The value of much writing on contemplation is to highlight an area of Christian prayer life and encourage us to move deeper in it. It means nothing less than this quiet, devoted gazing as an increasing part of our devotional lives. Notice that it is different from meditation. It is hard to do without some sort of meditation but over time someone can find themselves slipping more quickly and naturally into this less active state which is contemplative and quiet, like the child we thought about in Psalm 131.

How do we go about it? This is such a varied and personal thing that I am reluctant to suggest anything that could become a formula. However, like most people I appreciate practical suggestions so here are a few.

Contemplation is often the next step after meditation. In meditating on a bit of Scripture we explore its meanings and implications. It is like pulling the branch of an almond tree down so we can pick the nut. Then we shuck off the outside bits and crack open the shell. We put the kernel into our mouth and bite. So far what we have been doing is the meditation. Contemplation is chewing and savouring the flavour.

So contemplation means turning what we think we have seen, learned or heard in that piece of Scripture into a person-to-person encounter with Christ in which we move towards him in faith – perhaps with repentance, perhaps with gratitude, perhaps with intercession (asking him for something). Sometimes it will be a movement of faith – we've seen we can trust him about something that had been troubling us. Sometimes it is a movement of hope – seeing our future as one he has secured. Above all it will be a movement of love, for that is what Christ wants more than anything: the love which adores him and wants our wills to be merged with his will.

We make the movement and then we stay there. That is the point of contemplation – 'not rushing away' as the worship song puts it.[2] We stay there, gazing at Christ by faith.

Another approach is simply to start with Jesus and to fix our eyes on him (Hebrews 12:2). When I do this, I bring Jesus to mind and I think about some aspect of him. It could be his eternal existence of love with the Father and the Spirit. It could be his birth in the stable. It could be his kindness to needy people. It could be his sternness with self-righteous people. It could be his getting tired and thirsty and sad – all for me.

I often think about Jesus' death. When I focus on the cross, I do find that some mental image helps but I try not to get too focused on the detail. The most important suffering was not his physical pain (ghastly though that was) but his spiritual pain as he was punished in my place and went to hell for me. Simply bringing the cross to mind and staying there affects me deeply and connects at a deep level with all sorts of things that are going on in my life.

At other times I will dwell on Jesus' resurrection and his current seat at God's right hand. That is the perfect vantage point for directing operations for the universe and my life. Jesus looks down on me with interest and compassion. Then sometimes I think of how one day I will meet him face to face: his warm smile of welcome and his enquiry as to how I have used whatever talents and opportunities he has entrusted me with.

Sometimes I will mull over something less specific and more just a sense of the beauty and immensity of Jesus. He is an infinite being of unimaginable density and goodness – a being to capture my attention like the most spectacular sunset, the deepest gorge or the highest mountain shining almost painfully in the sunshine. I simply bow in awe and stay there, contemplating the greatness of Christ.

I can move from one to other of these methods and back again. However, the greatest personal connection seems to come when I settle on one of these aspects of Jesus and simply concentrate on that, all the time focusing on him as a real person who is really there and really is what the Bible says he is. The act of doing that rather than something else feels very important even though it is actually quite a passive thing – like a deliberate decision to be quietly receptive.

I suppose that each of us will have our own ways of

relating to Christ. I would not want to impose mine on you, any more than I would want to take a blueprint from my marriage or parenting or how I relate to my best friends and impose those on you. You can develop your own. And Christ wants to break through all the competition for your attention and to love you and know you coming to him in love.

Questions

What do you think contemplation would look like in your life? What could you do to make it a reality?

Prayer

Lord, I want to learn to contemplate you in your beauty, your holiness, your grace and your love. I find it hard to stop and do this – help me! Amen.

11

When it doesn't work for me

My wife, Debbie, and I have helped plenty of couples with marriage preparation and marriage enrichment over the years. We've used other people's material and even developed our own a little. There are basic principles that apply to all marriages as well as general practices that many find helpful. But each marriage is different so we always have to check that we are not overgeneralising.

I remember hearing about one engaged couple who did their marriage preparation with a husband and wife who were very keen on conflict management. Their own marriage had a good bit of conflict but they had learned to work through this practically with creative results. So their approach to helping an engaged couple was to give them a whole suite of tools for conflict resolution. The problem was that the second couple had very low levels of conflict so this wasn't much of an issue. Lucky people! But there were other aspects of their relationship that did need work because of the people they were, so help in those areas would have been useful.

In marriage preparation we encourage couples to think about their different personality types and understand each other. Tools like Myers-Briggs[1] and Love Languages,[2] if used as servants rather than as masters, can be very helpful, providing explanations for different people's behaviour. For example, why does he look at his watch so often at parties? Or what makes her jump up to answer the phone during family meals? (These are taken from my own marriage.)

How does this apply to prayer? Different sorts of people find different kinds of prayer relatively more natural or relatively more difficult. I have a friend who is an off-the-scale extrovert. For him the idea of a prayer breakfast with another guy is better than dinner at the Savoy. Because people energise him naturally, getting together with people to pray energises him. I suspect that spending time alone comes less easily.

Other people are more introverted. That does not necessarily mean that they are quiet or shy (though it may accompany those traits). It means that they are energised by being on their own. Being with other people is fun but tends to deplete them of energy. Therefore for more introverted people church services can include all sorts of good things but be draining, especially the informal chatting before and afterwards. People have very different levels of social energy.[3]

A Spanish psychiatrist and church leader called Pablo Martinez has examined the implications of all this in his groundbreaking book *Praying with the Grain: How Your Personality Affects the Way You Pray*.[4] His basic message is that we should make the best of the strengths of our personality type and work on the things that are more of a challenge.

The introvert should recognise that he or she has a natural bent to finding time alone. She can then find ways of working with the grain to use her natural 'replenishment time' consciously with God. But at the same time she should recognise that Christians are not called to isolate themselves and that times with other Christians will nurture both her and them. I have found that such folk can experience changes in their sense of wanting to be with other people as they learn to overcome their own assumptions about what will nurture them.

The extrovert, on the other hand, should exploit his love of company to the full, cutting with the grain that God has given him. The challenge is to make those times with other people spiritually focussed rather than just banter and bonhomie. A bigger challenge will be spending time alone in prayer but this can be worked on. It helps lots of people to acknowledge that they are going to find it harder than others to spend time alone regularly. Having that starting point can be rather liberating.

You could say that this understanding takes the pressure off a bit. It recognises that no one would expect them to find this easy or for it to come all that naturally. It shows that they are going to have to work at it a bit. They can reduce their expectation that they will be like their house-group leader or that church leader from history – mentioned by their preacher as a sermon illustration – who regularly spent four hours a day in prayer!

With that helpful reduction in pressure, the extrovert then needs to buckle down and just do it! What I have observed over time is that extroverts who do this make some interesting discoveries. They find that being on their own is not as dull, draining and even scary as they thought, most of all because God is there, and that is very energising. They find it is entirely possible to develop regular patterns and habits of solitary prayer in a way that they would not have dreamed.

Through persevering with their Bible reading and prayer, and repressing all those instincts to get going and connect with the world, the extrovert is changed. God works through that kind of self-denial, or rather God is working in that kind of self-denial. The life of the risen Christ is working out his patterns of prayer and self-forgetfulness in that person's heart. It does not necessarily feel ecstatic or even particularly supernatural but that is the point.

There are other personality variations that have an impact, for example the simple early bird or night owl difference. If you are the former, morning quiet times are likely to work better. That doesn't mean that an evening person can't have good morning quiet times, but they may take a little more work and a recognition that the individual is likely to feel less energised during them.

Here's another example. Several friends I have worked with like to take on a project. It appeals to them to think of life as a series of sections in which they deal with a particular thing in a particular way. I'm more of a slow and steady, repetitive person. So I have followed the same Bible reading scheme for more years than I can easily remember. But my project friends have several different ones in a single year. The same can apply to patterns of prayer.

Each person needs to work with the grain of their personality and then figure out if there is something to learn and take from the opposite personality. This will be beneficial, even if it feels a bit harder.

Questions

What is there in your personality that you can work with in your prayer life? Does the social energy aspect give an insight into your attitude to praying on your own or with others? Ask God to show you how you can grow both with and against the grain.

Prayer

Father, you have given me the personality traits I have. I want to accept them as your gift to me. Give me discernment in understanding them; keep me from self-obsession; help me to work with my strengths and on my weaknesses; and grant me to serve you with the whole of what you have made me. Amen.

12

When I drift away from God during the day

So far we have mostly been thinking about planned times of prayer – what are often called quiet times. For most people this will be ideally, if not always, once a day. But there is no reason to limit prayer to set times like that and good reasons why we shouldn't. In several places Paul opens things up a bit further:

… pray continually (1 Thessalonians 5:17).

… pray in the Spirit on all occasions with all kinds of prayers and requests (Ephesians 6:18).

This does sound a bit more than 10 minutes before breakfast and an hour once a month at the church prayer meeting! Many interpreters try to understand 'continually' and 'on all occasions' as pointing not so much to a continuous flow of prayer as praying being a part of lots of different parts of life. For example, we might pray at the end of an evening with Christian friends.

I am sure that is a good thing to do. Yet I wonder if other writers who want to see if they can grow into a more continuous sense of walking prayerfully with God through the day aren't onto something too. More mature Christians have written about it being possible for us to grow into a more 'moment-by-moment' relationship with God. But I think that is something that God will tend to give slowly and gradually over time to those who seek it, rather than it being something that is given automatically to all Christians from conversion onwards.

Is there anything we can do to nurture that moment-by-moment relationship? Yes, and as always there is an active side (what we do) and a more passive side (in which we respond to God).

First, the passive side. We can and should expect the Holy Spirit to be present and leading us. That is very clear from Galatians 5 and Romans 8:

> *So I say,* live by the Spirit, *and you will not gratify the desires of the flesh … But if you are* led by the Spirit *… Since* we live by the Spirit, let us keep in step with the Spirit *(Galatians 5:16, 18, 25, my emphasis).*

> *Those who live according to the flesh have their minds set on what the flesh desires; but those who live in accordance with the Spirit have their minds set on what the Spirit desires. The mind governed by the flesh is death, but the mind governed by the Spirit is life and peace …*
>
> *You, however, are not in the realm of the flesh but are in the realm of the Spirit, if indeed the Spirit of God lives in you. And if anyone does not have the Spirit of Christ, they do not belong to Christ … if the Spirit of him who raised Jesus from the dead is living in you, he who raised Christ from the dead will also give life to your mortal bodies because of his Spirit who lives in you…*
>
> *For if you live according to the flesh, you will die; but if by the*

Spirit you put to death the misdeeds of the body, you will live.
   For those who are led by the Spirit of God are the children of
God (Romans 8:5–6, 9, 11, 13–14).

As you read these key texts, you can't avoid the implication that the Spirit is active. He is not guiding us whether to put on red or green socks, nor even primarily whether to talk to Jane or John, or whether to be a doctor or a dentist. Instead he is leading, guiding, helping, nudging us towards faith, hope and love and above all *holiness*. So it seems to me that we should be open throughout the day to his leading – however it works for each of us. We should expect some sort of Spirit activity to prompt and nudge us towards these spiritual ends.

Closing ourselves off to this possibility is, I think, quite a dangerous move. I say so because I was convinced for a few years as a young Christian that such nudges and prompts were not part of the Spirit's work. The church I went to had a rather silly trend to claim God's guidance for every step of the day. In my scepticism I reacted too far the other way. I moved backwards in key areas of my relationship with God as a result. It took the influence of a couple of dear friends, including one who is now my wife, to help me move to something which I think is more biblical.

So that is the first, passive part of nurturing a closer walk with God. It is a genuine openness to the Holy Spirit moment by moment and a careful attentiveness to how he might nudge me.

What about the second, active part of walking more closely with God in prayer through the day? You may feel you have no time to pray because life is just too busy to stop. I have every sympathy because my life definitely feels like that on many days: meeting after meeting, going to and fro from work, shopping, cooking, washing-up, bedtime. But I have discovered that it is possible to reconnect with God in prayer during the day and that almost all of us do have moments when that can happen. Intrigued? Sceptical?

The reason is that most of us have smartphones. And most of us use those smartphones repeatedly during the day. Many of the times we use them we are not answering an important call or doing anything particularly urgent. We are filling in a 30-second to three-minute space which has opened up. I have invited lots of people to think about this honestly and almost all of them have admitted that their smartphone usage proves that they have multiple short spaces during the day. Is that true for you? Even if this particular example doesn't apply to you (you may not own a smartphone or use one during the day), I would still maintain that what I am about to suggest is eminently possible for you.

I recommend a brief, spiritually focused 'breathing space' throughout the day. Stuart Ollyot calls this a 'micro-sabbath'.[1] It is a very beautiful idea if we think of Sabbath as rest in the presence of God. You might pray in almost any way in this time, though it may vary from situation to situation.

Sometimes I pray the Lord's Prayer or the Jesus Prayer and am then quiet for a few seconds. I might repeat the Jesus Prayer, or might not.

Sometimes I realise I need to take stock of where I am. So I think about what has been going on: have I been depending on

God or myself? Is there some failure I need to ask forgiveness for? Are there some desires that need bringing under the cross? I find that last one important when I am shopping as, being the sort of person I am, I can find greedy urges to get the more expensive version or something I don't necessarily need. Or I pause to attend to a mood issue: am I feeling a bit uptight or miffed or apprehensive? I don't necessarily need to sort these attitudes immediately, but if I recognise and acknowledge them, I can then look at them in the presence of God.

Even more importantly this is a chance to realise the presence of God, as we have described in various ways in earlier chapters. I remember that he is only a micro-thin membrane away; that he is sitting very near me; that I can't see him because he is holding me so tightly. Doing that does not require a long quiet time when I have withdrawn from everyone else. I can do so anywhere and anytime. The key thing is that I respond when I feel that quiet nudge deep inside to move towards God rather than check my phone. For many, many people it is as simple and difficult as that!

When I do realise God's presence, I pay attention to some aspect of who he is: perhaps his holy being and his authority over my life, not simply that he loves me and protects me, though these truths may be what I need. These reflections are not simply to help me feel a bit better; they are to help me get back in step with the Spirit. They are part of what helps me join my will with Christ's will so that moment by moment I am choosing what he wants.

These micro-sabbath moments are times to refresh our

souls. In many marathon races drinks are supplied at key points along the course. In some water is squirted in a fine spray over runners as they go past. The spray does not go over the whole width of the course – the runners have to swerve under it. We need the same spiritually, and it can be ours if we swerve under the spray or pick up the drink as we go.

In the early days of the civil rights movement in the USA a boycott of public buses was called in Birmingham, Alabama to protest against racial segregation. Many, many African-Americans had to walk miles to work and back every day as a result. An ancient woman known as Mother Pollard was among them. Her minister tried to give her a lift because she was so old. She refused all suggestions that she should drop out of the boycott: 'She said: "My feets is tired but my soul is rested." It became a classic refrain of the movement.'[2]

I am convinced that this same spiritual refreshment is more possible for us than we think. We should engage with God moment by moment, taking deliberate micro-sabbaths through the day. This will then grow gradually in our lives until it becomes more and more normal.

Questions

Do you agree that biblically it looks as though the Spirit is active in nudging us towards holiness through the day? If so, what is your actual experience of this? How might you be missing out on his quiet leading? What could you do to extend it? What would it look like for you to enjoy spiritual breathing spaces during the day?

Prayer

Holy Spirit, I don't want to misunderstand how you work but I also don't want to shut you out and just operate on my own. Do your work in me. As for my phone, yes Lord, I really do want to connect more with you and less with my social media feeds. Help me. Amen.

Conclusion: When it still feels like hard work

Having got this far, why not take stock and look back at how everything you have read has affected your praying? It can be so helpful to be attentive to what God has been doing (because our prayer is supernaturalised). I hope that you will have felt some changes. What are they?

- Did you try praying the Lord's Prayer?

- Did you try saying the Jesus Prayer (or another short biblical prayer)?

- How did the chapters on meditation and contemplation affect you?

- Have you developed new ways of talking to yourself when you don't feel like praising God?

- Have you learned to move towards God and to stay there?

- If you found it hard to ask God for things, has that changed or has the way you ask him modulated into something deeper? Are there practical steps you have taken with lists or even apps?

- Have you tried drawing near to God in odd moments of the day? What have the 'best' of those been like?

Why not now try doing what a friend of mine does: he lists his overriding impressions from and the key messages of what he's read. What would they be for you here?

Then why not ask God to reinforce and take that work forward with a prayer like this:

Dear Lord, something has happened as I've read this. Thank you. I want you to take me forward into the next step. Amen.

But perhaps even the new practices are starting to feel like hard work? If so, this final little dialogue between an older and younger Christian might help:

I knew it.

Knew what?

That it would be the same old thing.

Same old what?

I get a new idea and a new impulse to pray for. I try it and for a bit it feels great. Then it starts to feel a little routine again and often it's just hard work. I am tempted to give up.

Poor you, that sounds pretty discouraging.

But what about you? You always seem so bright about

---

praying!

(laughs) Well, I suppose I have grown a bit in prayer over the years, but honestly it is often just plain hard work. I have to make myself open Operation World's daily suggested prayer for a persecuted country. I have to make myself work through the church prayer lists. And at times it feels like a wrestling match.

Oh great! I thought I would get past all that!

Nope. Not in my experience. After all, Paul's friend Epaphras had to work really hard to pray for the Colossians and it felt like a wrestling match for him too.[1] But I find that God gives me a bit more energy for the fight! And as habits get better established, it feels more natural to pray at roughly the same time each day.

But can't I expect it to get to the point where it is just like a ball rolling downhill?

Not really. A lot of it is just doing the same routine over and over again, with tweaks and changes to inject a bit of freshness.

I was afraid you would say that.

Sorry! But things don't stand still. Prayer is relational. It is not just an exercise routine; it is about me and God. The Bible is so clear that my relationship with him is dynamic, even though the ways that works are often hidden and virtually invisible – because it is lived out in faith not sight. I have found that if I believe that and I keep trying to pray, things do change. And as I press on with the routines and look to find ways of developing them or adding to them, there is a deepening relationship that is real. There really is the prospect of growth.

Amen!

Notes

1. When I don't know how to get (re-)started

[1] It is worth clarifying that though he gave us the model of the Lord's Prayer, of course Jesus himself never needed to ask for forgiveness.

[2] There are any number of good books on the Lord's Prayer. My favourite is by Peter Lewis: *The Lord's Prayer* (Paternoster, 2008).

[3] Abbot John Chapman, *Spiritual Letters* (Burns and Oates, 2003), p. 25.

[4] D. A. Carson, *A Call for Spiritual Reformation* (IVP, 1992), p. 19.

[5] D. A. Carson, *A Call for Spiritual Reformation*, p. 35.

[6] Abbot John Chapman, *Spiritual Letters*, p. 25.

2. When I don't know what to say

[1] *The Jesus Prayer* by Simon Barrington Ward (Pauline Books and Media, 2011) has really helpful bits as well as a long historical explanation which some will find interesting. However, I am wary of aspects of the ways it has been used historically, especially in the hesychast tradition which seems to me to have aimed at holy trances and altered states as if that was what a relationship with God was about. Of that I am dubious!

[2] The Navigators have a topical memory system that lots of people have found extremely helpful when memorising Bible verses and is something that's worth looking at if you'd like to grow in this area.

[3] Shaun Lambert, *A Book of Sparks* (Instant Apostle, second revised edition 2014), p. 135. This prayer is a powerful way of expressing biblical ideas of the love of Christ becoming more and more central in our lives, as seen particularly in Ephesians 3:14–21.

[4] 'A Liturgy for the Ritual of Morning Coffee' is taken from Every Moment Holy (Rabbit Room Press), copyright 2017 Doulas Kaine McKelvey; www.everymomentholy.com. Permission granted.

3. When I don't feel like praising him

[1] I think it is a pity that the 2011 NIV takes the 'O' out of this line, which in the 1984 NIV reads, 'Praise the Lord, O my soul.' Perhaps they thought 'O' sounded a bit old-fashioned but I often find myself saying, 'O Julian, you wombat!' (or worse) and I think it does represent the intensity of addressing oneself.

[2] See Matthew Henry's Commentary on the Bible on Psalm 103.

[3] Martyn Lloyd-Jones famously coined this expression in his sermon on Psalm 42 in *Spiritual Depression* (Eerdmans, 1965).

[4] See Matthew Henry's Commentary on the Bible on Psalm 103.

4. When I feel too rubbish for God

[1] Much of what follows is influenced by Alexander Ryrie's booklet 'The Prayer of Self Surrender' (SLG Press, 2007).

5. When I am too frazzled to pray

[1] God's use of feminine and maternal imagery here and elsewhere is very beautiful and important. It does not mean he is our heavenly Mother. But he *is like* a heavenly Mother in many respects.

6. When God seems invisible and distant

[1] Abraham Kuyper's book *To Be Near unto God* is still available in a variety of editions, including as a very low-priced e-book.

[2] Simon Walker, *The Undefended Life* (Simon P. Walker, 2011).

[3] I owe this image to Iain Matthew, *The Impact of God* (Hodder and Stoughton, 1995), p. 12.

7. When sadness or anger get in the way

[1] Graham Beynon, Emotions: *Living life in colour* (IVP, 2012), pp. 156–7.

[2] Peter Lewis, sermon on Romans 8
(available at www.peterlewis.cornerstonechurch.org.uk).

[3] Ajith Fernando, *The Family Life of a Christian Leader* (Crossway Books, 2016).

[4] Octavius Winslow, *No Condemnation in Christ Jesus* (originally published 1852; now available as an e-book), chapter 21.

[5] Raymond C. Ortlund Jr., *Supernatural Living for Natural People*

(Christian Focus Publications, 2013), p. 132.

[6] Martyn Lloyd-Jones, *Romans: Exposition of Chapter 8:17–39, The Final Perseverance of the Saints* (Banner of Truth Trust, 1975), p. 140.

[7] U2. "Mothers of the Disappeared". The Joshua Tree, Island Records, 1987.

8. When asking for things seems silly

[1] https://www.prayermate.net/

9. When Bible study seems a million miles from prayer

[1] There are good guides to how to interpret the Bible, notably *Dig Deeper* by Nigel Beynon and Andrew Sachs (IVP, new edition 2010) and chapter 10 in Timothy Keller's *Prayer* (Hodder, 2016).

10. When all I do is talk

[1] I am now going to sound like a stuck record but, once again, that is something that many, many books on prayer get very badly wrong: they make contemplation the privilege of a certain group, often monks and nuns. Even some truly stimulating writers can sound as though the greatest joys of contemplation are only for people who have disengaged from normal life and filled up much of each day with prayer. I don't think that is biblical.

[2] Noel Richards, 'To be in your presence' (Thankyou Music, 1991).

11. When it doesn't work for me

[1] Myers-Briggs is a widely used and influential personality test, assessing personal character traits on four different axes. One of these is Extroversion–Introversion, a measure of how much someone is energised or drained by being with others. See www.myersbriggs.org/my-mbti-personality-type/mbti-basics/home.htm?bhcp=1 (accessed 16 November 2018).

[2] Love Languages is a popular tool developed by Gary Chapman for analysing how each of us instinctively gives and receives love. There are five of these 'love languages': touch, affirming words, spending time, serving and gifts. See www.5lovelanguages.com (accessed 16 November 2018).

[3] Mark Dever pointed this out in a talk. It made me realise it was OK for me not to have *his* levels of social energy!

[4] Pablo Martinez, Praying with the Grain: How Your Personality Affects the Way You Pray (Monarch Books, new edition 2012).

12. When I drift away from God during the day

[1] This phrase comes from Stuart Olyott's inspiring book *Something Must Be Known and Felt: A Missing Note in Today's Christianity* (Bryntirion, second edition 2015).

[2] Taylor Branch, *Parting the Waters* (Pocket Books, 1989), p. 149.

Conclusion: When it still feels like hard work

[1] See Colossians 4:12.